GloryGram
Poetry

Peter H. Zipfel

GloryGram Poetry

How to Live God's Glory

Peter Zipfel

GloryGram Books

Published by GloryGram Books, Shalimar Florida, 32579.

Cover Photos by NASA Hubble Telescope.

First printing, February 2014.

Book > literature > poetry > religion > Christianity.

GloryGram Books; glorygram.zipfel@cox.net

ISBN-13: 978-0615963327
ISBN-10: 0615963323

Contents

Living God's Provisions 1

Living God's Glory 1

Beauty Visualizes God's Glory - A Sonnet 3

Blessings Apportion God's Glory 5

Joy Is the Evidence of God's Glory 7

Life Is Living God's Glory 9

The Kingdom of God Reveals His Glory 11

Mercy Flows from God's Glory 13

Grace Channels God's Glory 15

Music Resounds God's Glory - Sonnet 1st Ed. 17

Miracles Are Unusual Acts of God's Glory 19

Nature Exhibits God's Glory 21

Prayers Petition God's Glory 23

Reason Weighs God's Glory 25

Science Discovers God's Glory 27

True Art Interprets God's Glory 29

Truth Is the Reality of God's Glory 31

Gravity Illustrates God's Glory.. 33

Wisdom Articulates God's Glory... 35

Living God's Challenges 37

Glory Is the Substance of Accomplishments............... 37

Man Corrupts God's Glory... 39

Pride Usurps God's Glory.. 41

Sin Defiles God's Glory.. 43

Anxiousness Strays from God's Glory............................ 45

Trials Prepare for God's Glory... 47

Depression Lost God's Glory... 49

Boasting Promotes Glory.. 51

Boredom Misses God's Glory – A Sonnet....................... 53

Envy Covets Your Neighbor's Glory............................... 55

Fame Takes Credit for God's Glory 57

Materialists Ignore God's Glory 59

Self-Glory Demeans God's Glory....................................... 61

Music Resounds God's Glory – Sonnet 2nd Ed. 63

Fear Doubts God's Glory.. 65

Free Will Seeks Glory 67

Healing Applies God's Glory... 69

Compassion Administers God's Glory............................ 71

Humility Invites God's Glory... 73

Repentance Restores God's Glory 75

Death Liberates God's Glory 77

Living God's Fullness 79

Righteousness Trail Blazes God's Glory 79

Revival Drinks God's Glory 81

People Share in God's Glory 83

God's Word Verbalizes His Glory 85

Fasting Focuses God's Glory 87

Faith Enables God's Glory 89

Hope Anticipates God's Glory - A Sonnet 91

Love Consummates God's Glory 93

Wellness Is in Harmony with God's Glory 95

Goodness Promotes God's Glory 97

Holiness Beholds God's Glory 99

Praise Responds to God's Glory 101

Worship Experiences God's Glory - A Sonnet 103

Introduction

GloryGrams are *telegrams* dispatched from Heaven's telegraph.
They tell us to appropriate what God in all accomplished
Before the Earth was formed. These poems are my autographs
For you to live His glory, the works that He established.

GloryGrams bring *Gilead's* balm to you with peace and calm.
They speak about God's care for you, His manifold *provisions*;
Yet also touch life's *challenges*, how new hope may be drawn;
And culminate in songs of joy, the *fullness* of God's visions.

GloryGrams are *poesy*, I wrote in rhyme and meter.
Read them aloud all fifty-two, one per week each Sunday.
Revive your soul, refresh your spirit, take a time of leisure,
And join me, as I verse for you, to live in love God's glory!

SDG Peter Zipfel, February 2014

Living God's Provisions

Living God's Glory

The cry ascends to Heaven: "How should we then live?"
Was *chance* the midwife at our birth, the *fittest* seizing life?
Is all there is, we hear and see? That's all what life can give?
Are we condemned to turn to dust, to end our life of strife?

For all the span of man, these matters mattered most;
From Plato's *Summum Bonum*, to Nietzsche's 'God is dead';
With scientists explaining, that all is in your head,
It's up to theologians to ask the Holy Ghost.

His Word gives us direction, to follow Jesus' word,
He gave to His disciples, the Prayer of the Lord;
Which tells us to give praise—to God and Him alone,
While living in His glory, for now and evermore.

Beauty Visualizes God's Glory – A Sonnet

How beauty weaves a springtime band of blue,
About the mountains, meadows' mossy hue,
Enveloping the roses red renown,
Attended to by bees in shades of brown.
As I behold this beauty with my eyes,
The trees in green, the fields in furrows edged,
The sea up-churned, where seagulls soar the crest,
I thank the Lord for eyes that He has blessed.
They frame the windows of the wondrous soul,
And cast the colors, contours as a whole
Into the very essence of the soul.
Where beauty rises up to greet the Lord,
To praise His glory foretold in His Word,
The unsurpassed creation of His World.

Blessings Apportion God's Glory

Blessed is the man, who *delights* in the law of the Lord;
Who is consumed by the Word, which he reads and absorbs.
He is as a tree set by the streams of living water;
Bearing the fruits of the Spirit to bless each other.

Cursed is the man, who *despises* the law of the Lord;
Who is so vain to proclaim self-made laws to be whored.
Proud as a smokestack, he surveys the land to be won,
Spreading pollution around, till a bolt of lightning strikes him
    down.

Not so the *righteous*, who obey all the laws of the Lord.
You will be blessed in the city, the country, abroad.
God will throw open the windows of Heaven above,
And *you* will apportion His glory and love.

Joy Is the Evidence of God's Glory

Joy, the spark of godly glory,
Sets the heart aflame.
Burning all that is unholy,
Giving God alone acclaim.

Man absorbed in worldly pleasures,
Cannot feel this joy;
Feeds his body, fans his passions,
Fills his senses, grabs more toys.

Tired of his escapades,
He tries to please his soul:
Courage, justice, prudence—these
Virtues have his happiness as goal.

Yet, happiness and pleasure,
Leave the spirit dry.
God's own glorious presence
Alone brings the spirit joy.

Life Is Living God's Glory

The streets are damp and dreary,
The lamps are dim and scary
—Men scurry around,
To drown their empty days,
In boos, and games, and dames
—Where sins abound.

Why should I live in squalor?
I will avoid the parlor
—And mend my ways.
But life is full detractions,
In vain, I flee seductions
—I cannot change my days!

My life must change completely,
Exchange the streets for beauty
—Like move to Florida.
My new life is in Jesus'
Sacrifice that frees us
—Just live God's gloria!

The Kingdom of God Reveals His Glory

Kingdoms come and kingdoms go;
On Earth there is no lasting
Of man-made realms and worldly show;
Its rulers are but passing.

Kingdoms bear resemblance
To gardens growing, dying.
The gardener plants descendants,
Few prosper, most decaying.

Not so the Kingdom of God.

The Kingdom of God will last forever.
It was, is now, and is still to come.
It marks God's rulership far over
Heaven and Earth and worldly pomp.

God's desires are clear:

He calls us into His Kingdom and glory
By rebirth and living life worthy of God.
Then you have power to be His body
And carry His Will out on Earth as above.

His Will is established in Heaven above,
Its deeds stored for us in His Kingdom.
His Kingdom in us, by Jesus' love,
Revealed in us—all to His glory.

Mercy Flows from God's Glory

Surrounded by mercy, enveloped by love,
Are those who fear God and abide by His laws.
Though all we are sinners under sentence to die,
By Jesus' atonement, we're saved and alive.

Alive to do works that the Lord has prepared
For us to extend to the people ensnared.
To those who offend, we forgive—willingly,
And bear every wrong without wail—patiently.

Jesus said on the Mount:
"Blessed are the merciful,
For they shall receive mercy."

Mercy from God, the judge of all people,
Who, without mercy, judges the merciless.
But has compassion on those who are gentle,
Raining His glory from clouds of forgiveness.

Grace Channels God's Glory

Grace is the channel of God's love;

Love is the essence of God's glory;

Glory is the radiance from above,

Granting grace to you and me.

Music Resounds God's Glory –
Sonnet, 1ˢᵗ Ed.

Much sound surrounds us everywhere we go.
We meet it in the borough's bustling pubs,
While outside, autos tooting to and fro.
Yeah, all such sound suppresses music's touch.
We sense the sound of music in the trees,
With whip-poor-will's nocturnal call for rest.
We feel the roaring ocean waves of seas,
With seagulls squealing, soaring up the crest.
Then we escape in search of harmony
Into the hallowed halls of symphony.
Or find the balm of Gilead for our souls
In sacred music—all that God extols.
Yet *all* these sounds and music chords,
Resound the glory of the Lord.

Miracles Are Unusual Acts of God's Glory

Lord, I need a miracle,
The doctors cannot help me.
Pain shoots up my ventricle;
Is this the end of me?

Jesus healed the sick and dying,
Restored the sight of blind men.
Dried the tears of Martha crying,
Raising Lazarus again.

Lord, where is my miracle,
A special touch from You?
I need an act unusual
That doctors cannot do.

Miracles are acts of God,
Which we encounter seldom.
They are not like the promenade
The sun makes—just as awesome.

All His acts are marvelous,

Each is a special sign.

The rare ones we call miracles;

Where, oh God, is mine?

Nature Exhibits God's Glory

"**Here is a Picasso**, there is a Monet;
Look into that corner, Rembrandt's own portrait."
Up and down she struts, pointing at each oeuvre;
Hollers out the guide, echoes through the Louvre:
"See the cubic forms, feel the eyes set skewed!
Breathe the painted rags—*divinity* imbued!
Can't you see creation, right before your eyes?
How the masters garner glory from the skies?"

The air gets thick and heavy,
Her bombast makes me dreary.
Out I go for purity:
Au Jardin des Tuileries !

The blue beyond the gate, receives me with delight.
The greens of trees and brush, embrace me with a hush.
Look here, in the rosarium, how colors stir the light;
The Gloria Dei rose, retouches pink with white.

Oh Lord my God, how awesome are the works Your
   hands have made:
The speck of dust, the fish streamlined,
The trees up thrust, the stars arraigned.
The universe is Your display and nature fills Your canvas
—With glorious sights of allness.

Prayers Petition God's Glory

Saintly prayers rise before the throne of God.
Bowls of incense spread the sweet aroma
Of petitions, intercessions, supplications;
Swirling upward, touching God Jehovah.

God the Father, pleased with steadfast prayers
Of the faithful, activating His assurance
That His Will be done on Earth as is in Heaven,
Speaks the *fiat*: It is done!

All that God will ever do, already He accomplished.
God, transcending earthly time, has kept these works in glory.
The substance of His glory, on Earth will be established
Through prayers of His saints, petitioning God's glory.

Reason Weighs God's Glory

Reason is a gift from God and language is its servant.
Reasoning sets man apart from fowl and fawn and fauna.
But reason is a cross to bear demanding explanations
Of life's distress and life's success and all its contradictions.

Why does the storm destroy the house of righteous and
    unrighteous?
What crime an infant might be charged to die an early death?
Why people live in poverty, while others drown in surplus?
How justice is denied the man ensnared in liar's mesh?

These questions occupy the minds of earthborn sage and
    thinkers.
They lead to mental misery and end in desperation.
Because the mind and intellect are God's own precious
    treasures,
They should be used pursuing truth and not vain speculation.

Man's intellect, the greatest gift, employing thought and
    reason,
Unfolds the secrets of God's plan for life on Earth and
    Heaven.
It weighs the blessings and afflictions, perfecting us in season,
Concluding that alone His glory—effects our sure salvation.

Science Discovers God's Glory

I look around and am astound
Of nature's untold secrets.
Who will explain, who will acclaim
Their hidden glories greatness?

It's man who can pursue the quest,
To name and claim the stars;
To study life's descent from life,
And physics of the quarks.

These men are highly honored
By folks like you and me.
We shower them with accolades,
For all the World to see.

Most scientists are flattered,
And think that all that matters
Is science's Holy Grail
They worship and travail.

But then there are the men of God,
Who hold a higher honor.
They research nature and discover
The glorious works of God.

True Art Interprets God's Glory

Art is man's endeavor to recreate the World;
On canvas, wood, or copper, he fashions lifeless works.
A stave may be his pallet to scatter music notes,
Or he may be a poet and verses priceless quotes.

Oh how God's gift is trampled by self-proclaimed adepts,
Who bask in full vainglory by works of art inept.
Some even lend their talents to dabble in black arts,
And bring the devil glory by rendering their hearts.

But then there are the masters, who have been touched by
     Him,
To recreate His glory with canvas, stave, and quill.
The paintings of a *Rembrandt*, the music of a *Bach*,
The rhymes of *Robert Frost* bear witness of true art.

Truth Is the Reality of God's Glory

Searching in the dark of days
With blinders on her eyes,
Gropes truth about.

The search for truth, truth self can't find
Not in the halls of science;
Nor is it in the wide confine
Of nature's ever-presence.

Is all there is—Reality?
What I can see and touch?
How can the truth be found by me,
Without the Master's touch?

He came to us in grace and truth;
We have beheld his story.
Reality is found in Him,
The fountain of His glory.

Gravity Illustrates God's Glory

What mystery surrounds the common fact
Of gravity's unwavering effect?
It occupied *Sir Newton's* staunch pursuit,
And *Einstein's* esoteric search for truth.

Who knows its coming from and going to?
We only know it's here for us to do
Our walk on Earth, the tasks assigned to us,
As we obey its laws, to us entrust.

God's glory self is such a mystery:
We cannot make it, but die without it.
We cannot earn it, but violate it.

Yet God has given us all that he made.
So live His Glory fully as displayed
By gravity's grandeur—He arrayed.

Wisdom Articulates God's Glory

Philosophy, the love of wisdom,
Is held in high esteem.
In Plato's time, *Sophia* governed
The hearts and minds supreme.

Before that time, King Solomon
Asked God for extra portions;
And James, the Lord's companion,
Urged all to pray for wisdom.

What is this wisdom we confess?
Is it the *Summum Bonum*
Acquired through our life's duress,
Or academic forum?

True wisdom starts with fear of God,
The reverence of His glory,
Who shares His hidden secrets, stored
Since ancient times, for *our* glory.

There are three rungs towards wisdom's end:
    Information is data analyzed,
    Knowledge is information internalized,
    And wisdom is knowledge glorified.

God bares His works, so all can see
The glory of His majesty;
To know Him in their hearts,
Where wisdom *truth* imparts.

It's wisdom that articulates
Our righteousness in God.
In Jesus we have holiness,
Redemption as reward.

Living God's Challenges

Glory Is the Substance of Accomplishments

We all felt the joy of a job well-done.
Elated we received the praise of everyone;
And felt the weight of great accomplishments,
Become the substance of our own achievements.

The victory column of Marcus Aurelius in Rome
Portrays the *fame-and-glory*, *living-forever* syndrome,
That is expressed in modern times by the Nobel Prize,
Or Time Magazine featuring on the cover my face.

All this, our glory, is but a mirage
Of God's timeless glory, a camouflage
Of all His achievements, already done
—Before time begun.

All glory is God's, by which we are called
To be formed in His image, and be enthralled
By all the acts He performs through us
For His glory alone, and our fruitfulness.

Man Corrupts God's Glory

The weight of glory weighs on you and me
Of God's achievements for the human race,
Accomplished gloriously in all eternity,
For us to activate on Earth in time and space.

We have been given all we need for life,
The air we breathe, the hand to wield a knife.
But man, his soul corrupt by sin,
Applies the gifts for selfish win.

He smells the fragrance of the flowers' blooms,
As chimneys belching out their sodden fumes.
He wields the scalpel skillfully to save a life;
Another kills a rich man with his knife.

God's works are stored in Heav'n for us to claim.
How wicked if we turn God's glory into shame!

Pride Usurps God's Glory

Pride is like a potion,
A poison pill so potent,
That man abandons all,
His life and godly call:
To live a life of glory,
In God's own laboratory.

Man rejects authority;
Self-made is his priority,
To owe no one to trust no one,
To live in full autonomy.

Who needs a god? It's just a crutch!
I did it all, I know that much,
That all religion is out of touch.

When disaster hits,
Man foregoes his wits,
Plunging into fits.

All is lost!
Damn the cost!
I am bust!

Before the fall comes pride,
The root of evil's tide,
The cause of pain worldwide.

Pride usurps the gifts of God,
And grabs His glory as a fraud,
Instead of yielding to God's grace,
And be transformed to see His face.

Sin Defiles God's Glory

Still is the wheel of the mill.
Moss covered paddles are still.
Water has found another spill,
Tumbling down the hill.

Down at the lake, children are playing,
Painting the shore with their footprints.
Look, a small boy leans over, smelling
The baby-blue water hyacinth.

Way over there, across the spill,
Is another mill, milling and killing
Babies—their hearts now still.
And red blood spilling down the hill.

God created the hyacinth,
And boys to smell their glory.
But man, corrupted, full of sin,
Defiles God's glory.

Anxiousness Strays from God's Glory

Life abounds in unknown *unknowns*;
What will the tomorrow bring?
It is known by God's *all-knowing*;
We should trust in Him alone.

But we wander through life's jungle,
Straying from the sunlit path.
Fighting phantoms and then bungle
Into God's imagined wrath.

In the darkness we encounter
Sickness and the fright of death.
Will the airplane stall and flounder
As I suffer my last breath?

All these self-proclaimed disasters
Make us roving vagabonds;
Spurning light and peace, the Master's
Glory—What is your response?

Trials Prepare for God's Glory

Life without trials, like bread without salt,
Deadens the senses and keeps us apart
From the fragrance of Heaven, the glory of God.

Some trials of life are the testings of God.
He refines us like silver and turns us to gold
—The discipline of our Father, so we are told.

But not all trials are testings of God.

We may be bad stewards of body and soul;
My kinship with people may take its toll;
Or Satan may cast his spell from hellhole.

Whatever the trials, afflictions, or testing,
God works them for good, who truly love Him;
And prepares us for glory, a life of His calling.

Depression Lost God's Glory

Doom and gloom is all I see around me;
Soon there is no room for anything but gloom.
All my blooms are swept away by brooms,
Consumed by fumes and buried in my tomb.
Womb to tomb and in between a vacant vacuum,
Filled with fears and tears inside my soul's dim
darkroom.

Light has dimmed, my joy has fled;
Let me catch some drugs instead.

Drugs and booze are but a ruse,
Killing off what's left to loose.
All is lost at what great cost:
His love is lost—all is bust!

But did God really leave you?

You may not feel His presence,
     —but He is here.
You may not share His joy,
     —but it is near.
You may have lost His glory,
     —find it my dear,
And be set free from fear!

Boasting Promotes Glory

We start a conversation and listen to a story;
But do we really listen? Or think of our story
And how to interrupt, so we can tell our story
—And get all the glory?

To boast about our accomplishments,
Makes us feel good and important.
So what's wrong with some embellishments,
As long as nobody gets impositioned?

Why do you extol your achievements?
Don't you know they all are from the Lord?
It is He, who gave you the competence
To carry out His word.

Therefore, my soul will boast in the Lord,
And praise His glory in one accord.

Boredom Misses God's Glory – A Sonnet

We go through life's perpetual ups and downs.
Today we scale the mountains greatest heights,
Tomorrow finds us sloshing in the dumps.
Where is the joy that lifted our sights?
We wallow in the wasteland's weariness,
Is there no change to our dreariness?
I look inside and find but emptiness,
And grow in boredom and in tiredness.
What disregard of God's perennial gift
Of works, which He accomplished for us all,
To save us from ourselves, a life adrift
And give us purpose following His call.
So activate God's glory in your life
And boredom flees from you without a fight.

Envy Covets Your Neighbor's Glory

Blood was shed at first by envy:
Cain resenting Abel's blessing
Granted him by God Almighty,
For a sacrifice well-pleasing.

Envy covets what is not your own,
Be it riches, fame, or glory.
Yeah, the coveting of these alone,
Is but sin to God Almighty.

Fame Takes Credit for God's Glory

Fame lays claim to God's acclaim,
Grabbing all attention.
Grasping all to make a name,
Revered by every nation.

Fame feeds off the adulation
Of a fawning population.
But—take away the people,
Fame becomes a piddle.

All that public reputation,
Snatches credit, though it's debit
Of God's actions,
Accredited to man.

Materialists Ignore God's Glory

Science marches like an army,
Conquering the secrets of this World.
Scientists in trenches labor smartly,
Storming out with flags unfurled.

On their banner blazes but one word:
Matter is their only lord.
Nothing else is relevant in our world.

If I cannot touch or see it, it's not real.
Don't tell me there is more!
All religion is just make-believe;
To think it's real is just folklore.

Most scientists are blind of sight.
In darkness, they can't see the light
Of Jesus' glory and His might.

Self-Glory Demeans God's Glory

The World is full of wonders, of man's accomplishments.
High rise the mighty towers in cities through the land.

The man in penthouse ninety-five, surveys his realm of glory.
He built it, pouring out his life, all nine-ty-five stories.

"There is no greater tower,
As far my eye can see.
I have displayed my power,
For *all* to see."

The dark of night, the flicker of the windows,
Is conquered by the eastern sky.
The chariot of fire arises from the yellows,
To govern a new day.

The man in penthouse ninety-five
Is struck by the display
Of power, might and right
—To his own dismay.

"How tall I stand, yet how so small is this my edifice,
When I survey God's grand display, I feel so meaningless.
My glory comes from God alone, He is my life and call;
All else is rubbish and demeans the God I worship all!"

Music Resounds God's Glory – Sonnet, 2ⁿᵈ Ed.

As languages divide the human race,
So music weaves a band of unity
Around the souls of all humanity,
To lift us up towards a higher place.
I lean and listen to the sounds around:
The concert hall, the bar, and dancing hall,
Where men and women sprawl and are enthralled,
As high and low melodic lines resound.
They seek relief from stress and strain of day,
Embracing Mozart or Madonna as their way
To lead them into bliss, and flee dismay.
However short-lived is their desperate quest,
They miss the sound of Heaven so expressed
In music yielding to God's glorious rest.

Fear Doubts God's Glory

"No fear," is the war cry of this generation,
It is written on T-shirts and in graffiti.
"The only thing we have to fear is fear itself,"
Were the words of a president at war.

These words proclaim boldly our sovereignty
Over circumstances and the chances of life.
We are our own lords and serve no one;
Never mind what the Holy Scriptures say.

These men are fools without knowledge,
Because only the fear of God brings wisdom.
The reverence of our awesome God
Brings security and freedom from fear.

So why do you still dread the unknown?
Why do you tremble like an aspen leaf,
When death knocks on the door?

Fear God and Him alone,
And fear will flee your life.
All doubts of God's omnipotence
Are swallowed up in His glorious might.

Free Will Seeks Glory

Jesus came to set us free
Through truth, He taught to you and me;
And sealed His Will by His own blood,
To stamp out sin and all that crud.

So now we are like Adam,
Before the Fall and curse;
Sinless with endless freedom
Of Will to choose our course.

But what did Adam choose?
He followed Satan's ruse,
To be like God Almighty,
And grab God's holy glory.

That's your predicament too!
You seek what's not your own:
The glory for the deeds of you,
Which should be God's alone.

Healing Applies God's Glory

My body, afflicted with pain,
Cries out for relief from the curse
Of old, caused by Adam's disdain
For God's perfect universe.

With sin comes the punishment of God,
While Satan attacks the elect.
And man, his desires flawed,
Endangers his health towards shipwreck.

In ancient times no help was found.
A prophet, scribe, or psalmist
Could only show a future crowned
With the redeemer Christ.

He came to set us free from death,
The ultimate disease;
And on the cross with His last breath
He proved the truth that we are healed.

We are healed by God's provisions,
Fused into our constitution;
All the medical prescriptions
Are but balms of the physician.

It's the power of God's glory,
Granting everything for health.
Tap into His depository
And live a life of wealth!

Compassion Administers God's Glory

Compassion, Heaven's comfort for humanity,
Is both a godly trait and human virtue.
By God's compassion, Jesus gave us sanctity;
So we could share His love, and rise to rescue.

To rescue friends and next of kin from abject poverty;
To have compassion for the sick and pray for their recovery;
To comfort those that are distraught and suffer mental
    anguish,
Infusing God' compassion, so all distress be vanquished.

How can I have compassion, if I don't feel compassionate?
Must I experience shortage and sickness as prerequisite?
Let go my soul your sorrows! Apportion God's provisions!
His comfort is sufficient to heal all men's afflictions.

Humility Invites God's Glory

Humility an earthy term:
Of dust we're born and dust we'll kiss,
Save our soul that will live on
In deep despair or joyful bliss.

It is the soul that bears the burden
Of right relationship with God,
To open wide its heart and pardon
Its fellow man, though he be flawed.

The *hum*us of our existence
Should instill *hum*ility.
But our ego-deviancy
Demands divinity.

I want to be completely free;
Take pride what only I can do;
Yet envy those who better me
And covet what's another's due.

Instead, acknowledge God as master!
Take joy what He can do through you;
Thank God for blessing our neighbor;
Be grateful what He's given you.

To God alone we owe humility.
In Him we move and have our being.
Our fellow man is but our charity:
We owe him love, respect, and dignity.

God loves a humble, contrite heart,
Which invites all that He imparts:
The lifting up of our souls,
While sharing His eternal goals.

Repentance Restores God's Glory

Create in me a clean heart, O God,
Restore to me the joy of Your salvation.
Darkness has fallen on me as sin gnawed
On my soul and brought corruption.

Against You, keeper of my life, have I sinned.
Do not blot me out in the *Book of Life*.
Accept my contrite heart You have disciplined;
As I call on Jesus' sacrifice to free my life of strife.

Then a new day will dawn,
And the glory of the Lord will adorn me.
I will rejoice in my restoration, whereupon
God's glory is restored, and I am free.

Death Liberates God's Glory

The worst goodbye of all goodbyes is death the last goodbye;
To tear away from wife and kin, to leave behind old friends.
What once was one in flesh and blood with spirit soul, called *I*,
Now torn apart from time and space—though living never
ends.

What seems to be the end of all, is also new beginnings.
It is like leaving home sweet home to venture new
surroundings,
Or skydive from an aero-plane, relying on a chute;
—However scary the uproot.

Yeah, death is a departing, yet also an arriving;
It suffers separation, while promising reunion;
It causes life's destruction, but also grants new union;
And though there are much tears, there also will be cheers.

As I lay down my earthly gown and leave this time's confine,
I enter God's eternity, unshackled and set free;
To see the face of Father God unveiled and unconfined,
The glory of His majesty, the liberty for me.

Living God's Fullness

Righteousness Trail Blazes God's Glory

Righteousness a word of double meaning.
How it stirs the ego up inside of me.
Or does it humbly seek the outward leading,
Of God, who is the source of all integrity?

The man who follows all the laws of Heaven,
Has reason to be proud of his accomplishments.
He labors here on Earth to earn his mansion
Beyond, and craves vainglorious compliments.

But righteousness is not an earned commodity;
It is bestowed by grace from high above.
By faith it blazes paths into eternity,
Wrapped in Gods glory, reaching for His love.

Revival Drinks God's Glory

The modern World is like a desert,
Its World-Wide Web produces global sprawl.
The information split in tiny packets,
Is like the sand that permeates us all.

The sand piles high in all my gizmos;
I leave a footprint everywhere I go.
The winds of information overflow
Destroy my tracks, my alter ego.

We yearn for peace, yet find but troubles:
The heat of day, a stressing fierce barrage.
We make our world to match our morals,
A virtual sphere, a mere mirage.

But peace proceeds from Jesus in the desert,
His glory is our common bond.
Where our thirst is quenched by living water,
Revived by Him at His oasis pond.

People Share in God's Glory

The self-made man is self-contained, and owes no one
   his keep.
He prides himself in ownership of all that he achieved:
"I work to feed my family, and built for them a house;
I save to give to charity, and never beat my spouse."

We go through life as is ordained, and live with best intent;
We suffer loss and cherish gain, until the final end.
We live as if we were alone, and God a distant partner,
Who sometimes answers our moans, but keeps us as His
   paupers.

How little do you know of God's unbounded riches!
The freedoms He bestows on those He calls His own.
We live in Him, He lives in us in Trinitarian unity,
And shares His glory, all His works with us in glorious
   harmony.

God's Word Verbalizes His Glory

How glorious is the Word, that God has given us.

What power does it have, to set the captives free.

How far the message spreads, to angel's wings entrust,

To reach into the huts of Papua New Guinea.

There, the natives are in awe of sun and moon and earth.

They strike the drum and dance till numb to glory the new birth.

"All nature is possessed by gods!" So does the wizard spout.

To squelch their fears they turn and churn and bellow loud about.

The Word of God is brought to them by servants of the *Faith*.

They mold God's Word into their world and point them heavenward.

At last they understand, who made the sun and moon and earth;

And that the glory of the Lord is captured by His *Word* !

Fasting Focuses God's Glory

Fasting has become a relic of the past.
What was practiced by the monks and nuns of old
Has lost its meaning in a World that moves so fast,
Where time is short and prayer undersold.

So stretch your time with prayer and with fasting;
Declutter all your life in body, soul, and spirit;
And get attuned to that which is promoting
A closer walk with God, who rewards what's done in secret.

Lusts and cravings battle for attention in my mind,
Just like commercials pester me with offers of all kind.
Should I give in to them and get respite?
—Or walk away and be contrite?

The turmoil of the soul is stilled alone by fasting;
By concentrating on those things called holy.
Then like a lens that gathers rays of lighting,
Our hearts are focused on God's glory.

Faith Enables God's Glory

We all have faith that carries us through life,
On waves that swell from crests to troughs.
They lift us over rocky romps of strife,
And throw us down to sodden sordid scoffs.

What is this faith that we proclaim, which carries us through
    life?
Is it a gift that father gave, as mother strolled the baby cart?
It is acquired over time, in life's own strive and drive,
And then becomes internalized as bearing of the heart.

For some, faith is the confidence that stardom grants the
    actor;
While others trust in wealth and health, or lean on State and
    doctor.
Yet when the storms of life roar over them with might,
Their houses built on sand—cannot stand.

The faith that weathers all the storms is free, a gift from God,
Acquired by the willing soul that yields to God's command.
It opens up the Heaven's vault, with treasures spread abroad,
To live God's glory by His hand—and stand.

Hope Anticipates God's Glory – A Sonnet

Let hope rise up in me to greet the Lord,
The God of hope, who grants me joy and peace.
So I rejoice with Him in one accord,
As my despair relents, begins to cease.
No-hope in life is like a garden without seeds;
Each day I look for sprouts, yet find but weeds.
No-hope in life is like a cistern without water;
I raise the bucket, yet my thirst remains unquenched.
The farmer spreads the seed and hopes the best;
With Heaven's rain, his hopes will be fulfilled.
As we keep God's commandment, we are blessed
With Heaven's rain renewed, new hope instilled.
The hope we have anticipates God's glory,
The glory that fulfills all our hopes.

Love Consummates God's Glory

The mystery in human life is love.
Its presence brings delight, its lack despair.
We search for it on Earth, sometimes above,
But find it seldom, looking everywhere.

We look for human love and find but *eros*;
We make some friends and get but *phileo*;
We thirst for more and find the key in *logos*:
God says, my love, *agape* makes you whole.

We love because He first loved us,
So we can love our neighbor;
And give, what seems preposterous,
To any foe—the love of our Savior.

Love dwells in God's perfection,
The outflow of His glory.
Love is the consummation
Of God's salvation story.

Wellness Is Being in Harmony with God's Glory

Chronos turns the dial,
One more year has passed.
I am put on trial,
For all the care I sassed.

"Why do you shy the doctor?
When was your last exam?
Your colon may have the dodder,
Your spleen may—logjam!"

Fear haunts the human race.
What are tomorrow's bumps?
We hope for perfect peace,
But hit the dumps.

That is no peace, that man is fabricating;
There is no doctor, who can promise life.
The peace that passes all understanding,
Is only found in harmony with Christ.

A healthy body is in harmony with God's creation;
A healthy mind pursues divine intentions;
A healthy spirit yields to God's complete control;
Then, from God's glory flows the wellness of the soul.

Goodness Promotes God's Glory

The ancients searched for truth, and found but human
answers
To life's perplexing question: "What is it all about?"
It must be justice, courage, or wisdom, said the masters;
While Plato summed it up as *Summum Bonum* copout.

The Good, he said, a puzzle, my gods cannot unravel;
Nor can my lofty mind, the mystery untangle.
How little did he know, that centuries before him,
The LORD is called the *Good* in David's hymn:

"The LORD is good, His love endures forever,
His faithfulness continues through all generations."
As bearers of His image, we share His goodness' fervor;
And so promote His kingdom, His glory, and His power.

Holiness Beholds God's Glory

Who does not strive for wholeness,
A life devoid of inner strife?
To gain true peace and wellness
That guarantees a happy life?

But wholeness is elusive
Apart from genuine holiness,
Which is a life inclusive
Of God's unbounded blessedness.

How can a man be holy,
If God is called the Holy One?
Through Christ's redemption solely,
The sacrifice of God's own son.

Put on the new creation,
Created in true righteousness.
Become a newborn Christian,
And live a life of holiness!

Then you can sing with Moses
Of God's majestic holiness;
Beholding Him in wonders
Of all His glory's awesomeness.

Praise Responds to God's Glory

The glory of God is upon every son.
It governs his day, shining dusk until dawn;
Empowering life, giving joy to his toil,
Resounding in praise—no affliction can foil.

My praise is to God, giving thanks for my life;
My praise is for all that surrounds me in sight;
My praise for my mind, for the great mind of Christ;
My praise joining God in eternal delight.

Though nothing is added to God by my praise,
Since all is contained in His glorious ways,
I cannot but burst into joy—and raise
My hands to His glory, responding in praise.

Worship Experiences God's Glory – A Sonnet

The greatest gift that God has given us
Is granting us the joy to worship Him.
To live a life of love and godliness,
Ascribe to Him the glory due His name.
To know the splendor of His holiness,
Without Isaiah's fear of sinfulness;
We are redeemed by the blood of the Lamb,
To worship Him, the great I AM.
So worship Him in spirit and in truth;
For these the Father seeks, as Jesus said
At Jacob's well; and let the spring of youth
To dwell in you at Jesus' fountainhead.
Henceforth, I live my life to worship Thee,
Experiencing Your glorious majesty

Alphabetical
Contents

Anxiousness Strays from God's Glory	45
Beauty Visualizes God's Glory - A Sonnet	3
Blessings Apportion God's Glory	5
Boasting Promotes Glory	51
Boredom Misses God's Glory - A Sonnet	53
Compassion Administers God's Glory	71
Death Liberates God's Glory	77
Depression Lost God's Glory	49
Envy Covets Your Neighbor' Glory	55
Faith Enables God's Glory	89
Fame Takes Credit for God's Glory	57
Fasting Focuses God's Glory	87
Fear Doubts God's Glory	65
Free Will Seeks Glory	67
Glory Is the Substance of Accomplishments	37
God's Word Verbalizes His Glory	85
Goodness Promotes God's Glory	97
Grace Channels God's Glory	15
Gravity Illustrates God's Glory	33

GloryGram Poetry

Healing Applies God's Glory	69
Holiness Beholds God's Glory	99
Hope Anticipates God's Glory – A Sonnet	91
Humility Invites God's Glory	73
Joy Is the Evidence of God's Glory	7
Life Is Living God's Glory	9
Living God's Glory	1
Love Consummates God's Glory	93
Man Corrupts God's Glory	39
Materialists Ignore God's Glory	59
Mercy Flows from God's Glory	13
Miracles Are Unusual Acts of God's Glory	19
Music Resounds God's Glory – Sonnet 1st Ed	17
Music Resounds God's Glory – Sonnet 2nd Ed	63
Nature Exhibits God's Glory	21
People Share in God's Glory	83
Praise Responds to God's Glory	101
Prayers Petition God's Glory	23
Pride Usurps God's Glory	41
Reason Weighs God's Glory	25
Repentance Restores God' Glory	75
Revival Drinks God's Glory	81
Righteousness Trail Blazes God's Glory	79
Science Discovers God's Glory	27
Self-Glory Demeans God's Glory	61
Sin Defiles God's Glory	43
The Kingdom of God reveals His Glory	11
Trials Prepare for God's Glory	47
True Art Interprets God's Glory	29
Truth Is the Reality of God's Glory	31

GloryGram Poetry

Wellness Is Being in Harmony with God' Glory   **95**

Wisdom Articulates God's Glory   **35**

Worship Experiences God's Glory - A Sonnet   **103**

GloryGram Poetry

GloryGram Poetry